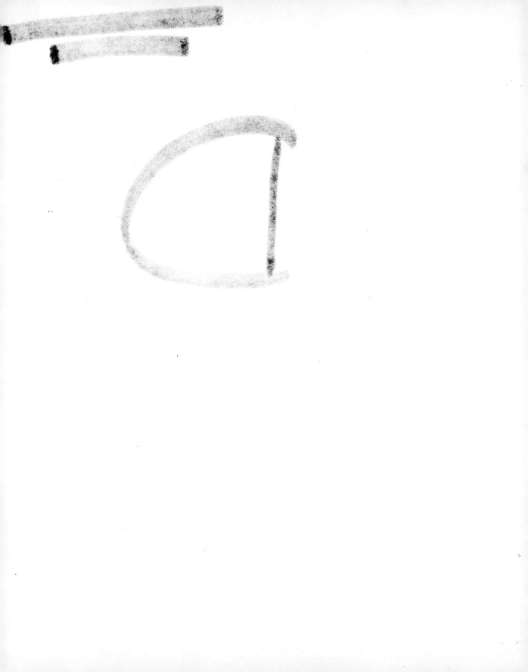

All About Sound

By Lisa Trumbauer

Consultants
David Larwa
National Science Consultant

Nanci R. Vargus, Ed.D.
Assistant Professor of Literacy
University of Indianapolis
Indianapolis, Indiana

Children's Press®
A Division of Scholastic Inc.
New York   Toronto   London   Auckland   Sydney
Mexico City   New Delhi   Hong Kong
Danbury, Connecticut

Designer: Herman Adler Design
Photo Researcher: Caroline Anderson
The photo on the cover shows a girl playing cymbals.

Library of Congress Cataloging-in-Publication Data

Trumbauer, Lisa, 1963–
   All about sound / by Lisa Trumbauer.
      p. cm. — (Rookie read-about science)
Includes index.
Summary: An introduction to the sources and characteristics of sound.
   ISBN 0-516-23609-1 (lib. bdg.)   0-516-25847-8 (pbk.)
   1. Sound—Juvenile literature. [1. Sound.] I. Title. II. Series.
   QC225.5.T78 2003
   534'.078—dc22
                              2003019067

CHILDREN'S PRESS, and ROOKIE READ-ABOUT®,
and associated logos are trademarks and or registered trademarks
of Scholastic Library Publishing. SCHOLASTIC and associated logos
are trademarks and or registered trademarks of Scholastic Inc.

3 4 5 6 7 8 9 10 R 13 12 11 10 09 08 07 06

Hello! Can you hear me?

Your voice is a sound.
A ringing telephone is
a sound, too.

Music is sound. Singing,
talking, and laughing are
also sounds.

Hit a drum, and what do you hear? A sound. A drum makes a booming sound.

Strum a guitar and you will hear a different sound.

Now strum a guitar again.
What do you see?

Look closely.

The strings move back and
forth very quickly. This
movement is called a
vibration (vye-BRAY-shuhn).

Vibrations make sounds.
You can see some vibrations.

Place a ruler on the edge
of a table.

Hold one end of the ruler flat on the table. Pull down on the other end of the ruler, and let it go.

The ruler vibrates.
The ruler makes a sound.

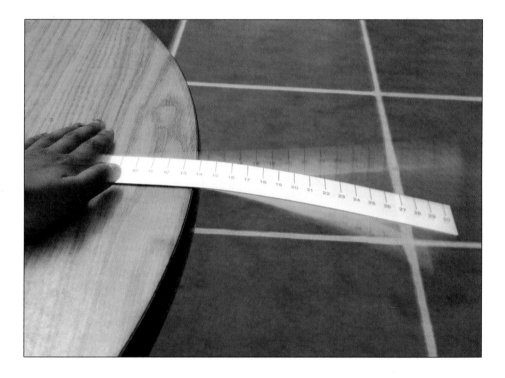

14

You can feel some vibrations. When you speak, your throat vibrates.

Put your hand on your throat and sing.

Do you feel the vibrations?

You can feel other sound vibrations, too.

Put your hand on a radio. You can feel it vibrate.

Turn off the radio, and the vibrations stop.

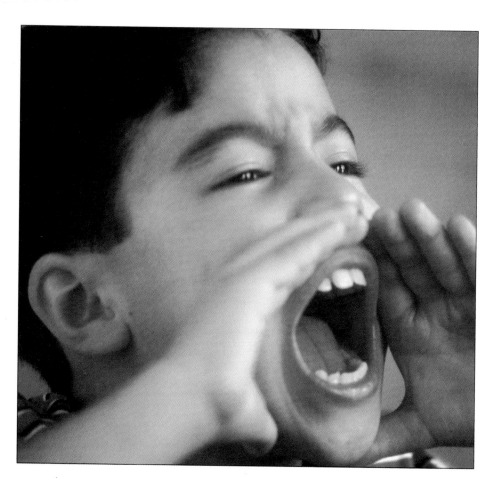

18

Sound can travel.

You can hear someone shout across the room. The sound travels to your ear.

Inside your ear, very small bones vibrate.

These vibrations send messages to your brain.

Your brain tells you what you hear.

Sound can travel through some objects. It can travel through a wooden door.

Sound can travel
through water.

Dolphins and whales
talk underwater.

Dolphins

You can make sounds, too.
Hit a pot with a spoon.

Blow into a whistle,
or clap your hands.

Guess what? You have made a band!

What other sounds can you make?

Words You Know

dolphins

radio

strum

telephone

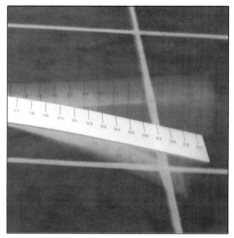

vibration

whistle

31

Index

About the Author

Lisa Trumbauer has written a dozen books about the physical sciences and dozens more about other branches of science. She has also edited science programs for teachers of young children. Lisa lives in New Jersey with one dog, two cats, and her husband, Dave.

Photo Credits

Photographs © 2004: Corbis Images/Jose Luis Pelaez, Inc.: 18; Ellen B. Senisi: 10, 13, 31 top right; Photo Researchers, NY: 7 (Jeff Greenberg), 3 (Richard Hutchings), 25, 30 top (Jeff Rotman); PhotoEdit: 9, 30 bottom right (Amy Etra), 5 (Tony Freeman), 21 (Richard Hutchings), cover, 6, 17, 26, 28, 30 bottom left (David Young-Wolff); Rigoberto Quinteros: 14, 22, 27, 31 bottom; The Image Works/Esbin-Anderson: 4, 31 top left.